The Morning

The
Morning

Roger Snell

Plein Air Editions ● Lowell, Massachusetts ● 2008

Bootstrap Productions
82 Wyman Street
Lowell, MA 01852

Plein Air Editions is an imprint of Bootstrap Productions, Inc.
a non-profit arts and literary collective founded by Derek Fenner
and Ryan Gallagher.

Plein Air Editions are curated and edited by Tyler Doherty
and Tom Morgan.

ISBN 0-9779975-2-9

Bootstrap Productions
www.bootstrapproductions.org
Distributed by Small Press Distribution.

To
Ann Marie
&
Duncan

Contents

One.

A stranger, for having been the object of his
own reading only, and for always, in his solitude,
reading himself in the words he reads.
                                        —Edmond Jabès

Pithy philosophies of
daily exits and entrances, with books
propping up one end of the shaky table—
the vague accuracies of events dancing two
and two with language which they
forever surpass—and dawns
tangled in darkness—
                                        —William Carlos Williams

Counterpane

1	"Look up & out" he sd
2	the sea what one sees
3	form (*is* as breath is beauty
4	(tender mast dance, act *is* self
5	the self / city plot, he walked
6	this night along the sea, stood there

7   here
begins
space

8   the place
is as (root
a plat

9   the city-
ship, how
return from
exile

10   the sea
a point well-
spring back

11   map, his
head-nest
flower / house
holds

12   *the long*
dumb dream
to speak

13   as eyes
self-things
the sea

14   is beauty
      what one
      sees as
      skope

15   *nescio quid sit*
      "I do not know
      what it is"

16   periplum / prairie
      top mast
      grass (in wind

17   as now, stood
      there, flowery
      earth-sea

18   looked up
      & out, to point
      beyond (back
      what one *is*

19   sea
      self
      love.

The Morning

I want always
(now) to go
away

walk beyond
the every
day

self, some
other view
to fill

this so-
called
space

This
side of
world

morning
faint traces,
night's last

moon, pitched
rows, sun
thru east

window
lines,
shadows

To be oneself once and for all
sometimes I don't want to be seen at all
else it is the room, walls

I is not I, nor here, the place is beyond
an unsure distance no clearness or
much purpose

The day was elsewhere
so I'd thought to go away, yet tendency
he warned to shut-off or out was there

Still the ground shifts, I'd read the day was gone
the room black, such enclosure to stay in,
inhabit act, destroy all instances

Day begins
house is quiet
next-door neighbor's out
sun below horizon
ocean's tide recedes, traces
movement, wreckage, split lines, outer
shore, upon these shelves the world opens
outward, turns in on itself

What I imagined was real was before me
unnamed, made-up, it is myself
no longer different then, the sense, but so often
the sound's a dream or want to be somewhere else

Sun in front room
light across wall
banister's shadow on floor
front door's open, inviting to all
look out upon world
people walking by, neighbor in window
hello world, I am here at home

Where was it?
it was in the air to reach after

What was it?
like boy when whatever turned me back
towards home was idle time

How did you know?
when I was younger I wanted to be. . .

out in the world
far away from home

distance increases
time's economy

until one is
possibly nowhere

Whatever space there was
one went far to see it—
Lookout Point, Fisherman's Island
Slippery Rocks—until looking back meant
any imagined self was beyond home

blue   solitary
some small place   outside
window
trees
light   time   morning

A shift or break
thru window (these yellow walls)
angle of sun, remember
pictures in next room
field, red house below,
grove of White and Norwegian pine

I want to see what lies
ahead, the shore
or some spit
to stand

Such enclosure
as the room or rise
to redeem oneself
and likewise
(find a) love

Like a mirror shooting back
Impatiently I

had gone the distance
to break the day

far beyond
unending bread

the dying night
of morning light

I walked away
waked

into the world outside
into scarce time

the blackness faded
to make

the place I called home
my peace with April

A Suite for Eva

Jimmy Juniper
& Tom Foolery
drink like fish—
two nights of debauchery.

●

Today plaster the
hall, tomorrow
doors to hang from
these same walls.

●

A typewriter &
piece of paper,
time alone, the
paint's whiter.

●

Friends from Holland
Gael Turnbull, Eva's
Mami for her birthday—
dinner's on.

●

Ah, a book—
plenty of pages
& poems, even
a picture to look.

●

As ever
poems surprise
all to game
adds flavor.

●

Lazy bugger—
two and half years
of sleep for
3 nights of tears.

●

We had it pretty good
in those days—
there between us
Eva lay.

●

I've grown fatter
from not smoking, my
hair's long & I've a beard
what does it matter?

●

Not so much a series
but little uns of similar
intent—a small window
to look out.

●

A picture to hang
next to yours so
you can see the
light in the evening.

●

Here reads hear
done needs blind
how we talk
is mind's ear.

●

A note merely
to cut possible
sentimentality
of home.

❋

One stone be-
side another—
Jasna and Eva
water the flowers.

❋

Rakes, shovels, hoses
a lawn mower—for
Eva's birthday, a
tiny garden shed.

❋

Enough to use
the word—
thinking there's
enough to go on.

Two.

The father's word is compassion;
The son's filiality.

— Ezra Pound

Evocation

Still, half awake

    song
    under cliffs

    (periplum—

Beyond, far reaching

    my ship
        (sense

        is drifting, headlong
this gam to cohere

      between men / words
        at hand, under hand

to heart & head, one word
    sound, some God

      creator
      preserver
      destroyer.

Place

How measure
>> heart & home

>>>>> as space to crawl inside?
>>>> To play as child in that fabulous
landscape is scale

>>>>> but you can't go home again.
>>>>>> What carries?

The marble cat
>> placed in garden, distant bell
>>>> in wind

>>>> some distance, mountains (overhead
OUTWARD thru window

>>>> I recall my mother
building a simple structure
>>> made from sticks.

>>>> Wooden floor, worn
>>>>> & corner stone

notched initials, low & gray
this night

   rises / sways
    slight drift
     backwards.

   To walk away
      as man in the mountain
  or boy on clouds is familiar.

    Where sound & silence
   are measured out.

Far from home:
    the wet leaf clinging
     to the door.

New Growth

I sketched the old man at eighty-five
        w / deep sockets
            & lines

    looking back to the year I was born

"To Joyce's grave
                at Christmas
        unadorned

            and Nora's
                there in the grass
            illegible."

        Then went for a walk in the night
            down stone alleyways

                past the café &
                manufactured columns
                    the corner bar.

At almost thirty
        what I possess is
    a great sense of angling in darkness

and recall
as I walk over the wood plank bridge
the Confucian virtue / image
of Ez

as an old tree enduring
in severe conditions

longevity
man
human.

Fatigue

Couched in cold earth
        under light snow
    & cat's paw

      a kernel (*Quercus robur*

        lies potent, broad-leafed
simply lobed, compounded in the pocket
    of Odysseus' hand.

In that swart ship he sailed, wrecked
      seven years with willing Calypso
      to cast off

      upon half bronzed decks
    & stretched sail (eighteen days

Taishan in the distance, Poseidon
      blasting waves & Ino with the lovely ankles
    veiled.

Stormy sea wine-faced sea
    (a blunder Rouse says)

       rode Odysseus astride a spar
    two days aloft on Athena's watery loft.

Spit out on land where the long
steep salita runs to
            Sant' Ambrogio.

Suppliant, naked & worn
       he did lie underneath
          a red-petaled canopy

above dropped spring seeds & a broad-leaf bed
       and heaped that fired seed away from prowling cats
     & called it memory.

The Effect
after Gaudier-Brzeska

Under halogen glow
　　　there is no break

　　　　　or gap, only a simple design
　　　　　of lines

& planes, stone-age
　　　metallic, a Mauser rifle

　　　　　pinched from the hands
　　　　　whatever comes near.

　　　　　A dropped leaf

young buck out of nowhere
　　　(Dordogne caverns

　　　　　periphery of vision
　　　　　forms a bas relief.

　　　　　　Broken at one a.m.
　　　　　　its clogged hooves

            silent as the trenches
this paltry mechanism

            quiet as the night
                it passes
                out of mind

gentle outline, a shape
            ((lines &

            black barrel
            muzzle.

Cold BLAST
            empty as I stood.

Three.

These are poems of an irregularity.

—Robert Duncan

I have a chair in the stairwell, just up under the stairs, by
    the floors-high window, to sit in the sun and watch the
    dust motes drift, the light flux
And I will carry the watch as a seal, burnt in and burnt out
    of the swirling column of extracted lives, and mine.

—Ken Irby

Eighteen Views

but from the hearth stone, the lamp light
the heart of the matter where the
house is held
—Robert Duncan

Night's gone under
morning's begun

colors blur
dreams too.

I am who sits here
a flicker, a flame.

◉

This day blooms auspiciously in gray
air gets lighter, houses take shape
the people in them.

Strangers in a
strange land.

My California.

◉

Where's the fact
of it, the faces
or as a friend says

"so unclear
from the start."

●

. . . *the actual is the drawing of the face—*
and so the face borrowing of the drawing—
by lack of copying and lack of a burden to
the story—is real.

●

One tracks his
own life:

wife, child
& cat.

Four rooms.

●

Fog's thick, the mind
cloudy, body tired
and restless.

Ann's in the bedroom
sleeping with Malki
at her feet.

Her breathing's more
labored at twenty-
three weeks.

◉

JP, Jasna, Eva
in their new home, far off
in Cornwall

Language we
think
           means
that we
do

I want their faces with me.

◉

Crazy how the fog
moves, settles—

When snow falls the flakes

rise up, swirl around
home & hill

spin upon the long axis

slip into some other
shape, a dance

that concerns them most intimately

of dissolving elements
a study in pale gray light.

●

Remember on first moving here
Those mornings when you were young

looking out the window in front room
the world gone under a layer of snow

I saw (I believed) snow thru Eucalyptus
you'd lie in bed waiting to go outside.

●

Days like this I'd walk
out the door (as Bashō & Sora)
and not look back until
myself was suddenly gone.

●

Ann's in shower, rivulets of water—
the liquid and rushing crystal—
over face, legs & back.

Love's first
glimmer—Summer
Evenings—

postcard on wall (1947)
a screen door,
rain.

◉

Trace—
passages of
the mind

out of time
to simply move
beyond

fragments, words
where our acts
are located.

◉

I'm either in my head
or outside of it.

Did someone say that?
Haven't I been this route before?

●

Think
of the words
now & away.

Ann now walks
into the kitchen.

To go away is equally real
to depart to where I am.

●

Sun breaks thru fog
a ray of sunshine in this other world

under world
un done word
un der wood
underwear.

What are these elations I have.

●

Outside—
dotted houses
                against green
hills, wind thru gray mist
                white sails
                        in sun glitter
                Mt. Tamalpais
                        over blue seascape.

                        ◉

Dale's "January Resolutions" rings in my head—

the expanding light
moving within the house
Hoa & Keaton—

"I will watch carefully for the Red-Crowned
Pine Grosbeaks who take thistle from the feeder."

Dear Lengthening Day . . . .

                        ◉

It all returns home
such deliberate
words as action

*What I aspired to be
and was not comforts me*

A wife
a child
a house.

The House: A Domestic Novel

Perfect note. Rain.
"Soughing Wind Among Eucalyptus."
Condensation.
One window.
To look out.
The song goes.
Just this day.
Sweep floors, cook.
My practice is nowhere,
my opinion is here.
Half wanting to be social.
Pretend.
Clean surfaces.
Books on desk.
Familiar order.
This room.
House.
Many hills.
The train below.
Lost in sea mist.
Golden Gate.
A so-called study.
Fragment.
Cat on windowsill.
Cup of coffee.
Floorboards bitter cold yet functional.

Much like childhood.
It's a chilly winter day.
Time to go out & play.
Paths & woods.
The "Original Impulse."
Clouds roll by as
shipwreck silent in winter.
Visibly light outside.
Constant flicker thru window.
Dotted houses in distance.
Wood smoke.
Drifts like ambition.
"A succession of endless subtractions."
Bowl of oranges.
Canvas of yellows.
Thin sliver of light on wall.
Otherwise pathetic with four rooms,
yet attractive pacing back & forth
across hall. Collect spare change
vis Komachi's "squandered
hours gazing at the rain."
Bits & pieces here.
Repetition. Day's lily like this.
Three figures.
A perfect recipe for home.
Numerous drafts "scrappy as hell."
Woven curtains.
Geometrical daydreams.
A lamp lowly lit.
Paper. Sleeping child.

Winter day.
Gathering divers impulses.
Across threshold of door.
Blue sky. Blackberries.
Cars audible in the sense of
not wanting to be seen.
Topographical.
As reflex, rough edge.
Roof's peak.
Saturated.
In sun.
Clearing.
Ocean's timbre.
Time's passage.
A table between.
Two chairs.
Blue pepper grind.
Sun's reflection apropos
Schuyler's cup—
"two boys, a dog and a
duck."
Nursing mother.
In half-light.
This story.
Shifts upon her
as blown clouds.
Sutro Tower.
Coastline.
Mind roams.
Hopper's Summer Evening.

A warm base.
Turns of phrase.
Less employable at every turn.
Soluble, whitish-gray.
The forecast.
(There is wind space
& rain space here.)
Cut out.
Blue print of day.
The light of things.
Stirs. Morning air.
My child in the arms of his mother.
We're alone quite beautifully.
A documentary of sorts.
Marginal on this hill.
The sea beyond.
See, how gorgeous the world is
outside the door!
Quiet now as the day progresses alone.
Letters pile up.
Children on their way to school.
To gather intelligence.
Similar to C.I.A.
Rosemary blooms.
"Where's the you
you of yr poems?"
The unformed lump.
Common when
tongue flaps.
A tough nut to crack.

A stick-in-the-mud.
The saying goes.
Diaper service versus mail.
What can be said today?
"All seems superfluous depending
on the moment no one will read it."
The average price of failure.
Reduced from originals.
Rather isolate.
Flecks.
Think of Joanne's
A glove exactly fit like one's own life.
The difference sensible
in the tone.
Is place.
Home?
Winter's house.
Light on floor.
As Duncan sleeps.
Walls fade.
Last night's rain.
Green hills.
A toy boat.
Woods around pond.
To wander again.
A bell at dinner.
Sun, clouds, stars.
Tide pools.
Far-off edge of sea.
Oppen's wooden corners.

Day's ordinary activities.
A vibration in the ear.
The human eye.
An outward negotiation
of fact not psychology.
See it on the page.
Thinking, thinking.
Nothing is known.
"Perfectibility in rough strokes."
Echoes. Yesterday's airmail.
Jupiter.
The Greek pun about how
the moon's light
is not its own. (See notes.)
Roast eggplant, shallot, garlic, onions.
Blue ball cap on doorknob.
Back of kitchen window.
Our small world.
Words. *Is.*

Seven Days

i.

Tuesday—

morning rain
remember sunlight
particles

a slice in space
geometry of memory
his tiny hands

their motion
thru air
how they move

as melody, as
essay, as
architecture.

ii.

Sunday—

think of home
as gesture, as verb

light between
two bodies

watch him point

out open window
to Oppen's

jagged hills
trees beyond

primitive woods
of youth.

iii.

Monday—

Square patch of sun-
light thru transom

blue sky, neighbor's
two year old girl

outside. Lists, stacks
files, it all fades

away. Thinking
mind's still, thinking

someone's out there
talking words

"I was talking . . ."

how the image
reflects life's light

love in the eyes.

iv.

Thursday—

Sun light thru
eucalyptus

Lights upon the
place we are

Sea glitter
star of Jupiter

The distances

Our small
imperfect world

Between elements
my love

The small words.

v.

Friday—

just beyond
water's edge

lap of wave
each syllable

fore-sheet
taut, a final

pull, refrain
word—

mother & child
single note

counterpane of
dissolving flesh

morning celebrants.

vi.

Wednesday—

single glass pane
Duncan's handprints

against lamp glow
white frame of window

black shifting mass
morning's gray edge

opens beyond
uplift of hill

like when I was a boy
light lifted one's

body to float

away, a cloud
a bird, a star.

vii.

Saturday—

"light being
morning distant"

horizon a
thin line

on typewriter
in middle of room

locality of
small words

The short night—

this loneliness
to covet

leap into
splendor

sun beyond sun beyond sun.

Song

Not I but
someone
way out there

at home,
beyond snow
capped peaks.

You who stayed,
were *heard* in
a dream

which so
completely
is forward

in time,
location,
awkwardness.

What do
you insist
upon?

A geography
existent, clean
surfaces.

Daily the
world
accumulates

outward. A
figure in
quiet.

Careful
song, so
beautiful

in grace
the point then,
to write (this).

Four.

This "still-here" of the poem can only be found in the
work of poets who do not forget that they speak from an
angle of reflection which is their own existence, their own
physical nature.

-Paul Celan

I sit at the family table where it's a struggle
To create both staminate and pistillate in the same
Inflorescence of cluster

-Bernadette Mayer

Vertical passage
light-wedge
edge of window
looked at in reflection—
light on across street
cat by door
This still here
dog-eared phrase
this angle
lost in craft
this slow day going

●

Ann & Duncan asleep
Sesshu's Long Scroll
veils & mists
a constant theme
pleasant to walk around
this word-compress
these undulating
hills of green
stone foundations
thru wood (absent
this far west

●

this half-light
of mineral wealth
lower earth
of value, this
encounter
insular drift
inward draw
seed translation
laboratory of poems

◉

lost car comes
in on the morning
light, off reflecting pool
of Creeley
quiet as is proper for such places
this space between
each bale of words
a fistful of green shoots
tansy on hill
fissures of blue

◉

we inhabit four rooms
a series of forts made
from discarded fabric
measure light
descending
thru Eucalyptus
dappled sunlight
on wooden floor
there's a lot of lacto-fermentation
going on in this house
this city squeezes it out
like a Fanny Howe poem
green leaves are like pages, waterized

                    ◉

to be simply moved by
dispersal of light
books & papers
spines just read
on desk—
my dream diary
is blue
"I read it tangled up
in sound sense
of the language
more than logical"

                    ◉

a spongy dream reflection—
I carry the sentences
lug them up
this hill
a bundle of sticks
for the fire
sirens in distance
sea far-off
cliff swallows
skiff on waves

●

Ann's portrait
by dried flowers—
apparent as light
enters room
the edges
where lines
blur, press
upon letters
outward into blue sky
this would be a novel
if the names were invented

●

Jewitt's covert journal
written in blackberry juice
Great Blue Heron
on neighbor's roof
a carousel of simple words
in far corner—
the installments
secure ring of wet
glass from water
the apple pie cools
off by window
in all the stories

●

tree's line margins
yellow grass to sea—
summer is a handbook for children
the locust singer
reproduces sound of cicada
a leg-of-mutton-rig
does not kick up
pictures in people's homes
do become what they say
as Williams sd

●

Melville probe
this morning—
infinite Pacifics
pagoda of self
word-traces in air
foxhole-combat
porous odors
from sawed-off sentences
leak into dustbin
of half-notes

●

no word-flow today
without slippage—
beyond reading ambitions
I look outside for
kitchen activity
discernible edges
transfixed by
this fire
above
us

Aperture

Mine—
to let light
thru plumb
line

●

Think be-
ing home
each room
sorted

●

Variations—
a play on
Williams, a
sequence of days

●

This quick
reply mirrors
the afternoon
· gone by

●

Mend leaky
tap, the line
to know / mind
needs no gap

●

Loss—
is the first
draft, is
sounding

●

Read *Gone*
in bed, the
bright sun,
orange light

●

A daybook
wedged a-
gainst this
window ledge

●

Poems from
home, care
makes
habit

●

No rest or
drift just
these epistles
to please

●

Drop titles—
pages, a
plenum of
of / or / from

●

Yes, a book
solid & tight
poems set
right

●

Eyes & ears
where they
are, yr lines
cohere

●

Off cuff
cut dross
drop this
from song

●

Rain is
as mind
reads to
find light

●

Se-man-
teme, a-
line w /
clear ear

II

I think of
open windows.
White blossoms.
Winter's interior light.
The submerge.
Of contours.
A penumbra.
This night-verge.
Dream life.
Solitude. A.
Syntax.
Flowerlight.
The lamp.
Curve of.
Orange rind.
The silences.
Inside the.
Passage. Marked
by. His hand.
The dusted.
Surfaces.
White luster.
Well spring—
"Back. Map.
Head-nest."
Word-trace.
Becomes.

Cornea & sclera.
Celan's *eye orb.*
The blue.
Cornice. A-
long margins.
Threaded folios.
Gleam against.
The casements.
This loneliness.
Gimme something to eat.
"to repel all idiots."
Bashō's humble fare.
Small words.
For assemblage.
Excess.
Thresh it out.
"This unending night.
That's left to sleep thru."
These passengers.
Of obsession.
In adjacent room.
Whiz along.
Drive he says.
On the simplest of means.
The possibilities.
Accumulate light.
The angular.
Movement.
Of words.
By dead reckoning.

As branch artery.
Become mirror.
A glass negative.
"The blood of night."
The wind.
Ay!
A kaleidoscope.
Spiral jetty.
Candle-flicker.
Incandesce—
"Light breaks.
Upon the floor."
This atrium.
Of the heart.
These letters.
What we read.
Enters the story—
This white light.
Blue night.
In the city.
Box-like.
The edges.
Tremble.
Reflect.
Bent rays.
Of moon.
Of the.
Spent hours.
The night-
hewn lines.

Lopped off—
Flung as-
under. At
four a.m.
Corresponds—
This gloss-
black stria.
Vertical dance.
Self portrait.
On the word-
strewn floor.
Hey diddle, diddle.
The moon is just an-
other place like
California.
A Serpentine Ridge.
Single window.
To look out—
A series of.
Of hills.
Of stacked clouds.
A Cloud Terrace
Mountain.
Three realms—
Magenta orchids.
In the lamplight.
The light-
belt along.
Parnassus Heights.
A word-plot-

torque-wheel.
Presses. The
Edge. Of
this. White.
Space. Above.
The incoming.
Fog evidence.
Ink smolders.
The syllables.
Condense. A-
mong bush
lupine. And.
Franciscan
wallflowers.
This oblique
projection.
Enters. "The
chase. Of
letters."
Thru window.
A divided.
Reflection—
tracery.
Rosebright.
In the cap-
illary action.
Moon's ob-
long. Drift.
This meridian.
At the Cut.

Is merely light.
Sun glimmer.
The tones.
Of light.
Adaptation.
A. Cartography.
Of.

Song
for Duncan

Limn mineral
artery, rifle thru
dappled sun-
light, this
blue essay
word-machine

◉

Display variations—
the wisteria
in common
room of mind
heart's in-
candescence

◉

The blanched
serifs taper
the complexities
between lilied
fields & wooded
emblems

◉

Inflorescence—
a branched
alphabet, a
tessera for
Williams'
lost g

●

Light-drift
upon trellis
a gold reflet
against green
tendrils, flat
detail of pea

●

Lucere
to shine
cluster of
red poppies
cobalt halo
around stone

●

Eye-bright
flower-head
ecliptic—
sun-flash in
"the aortic arch"
light-blood

◉

Of the muses—
mind-flare
suspended in
pollen, this
sepaled word-
theory

◉

Arc of c
divergent, light-
fold, radian
of composite
hieroglyph—
spiral sweep

◉

Atria—
heart-sun
white-ringed
chrysanthemum
vein-blue
nimbus

Elide—song

Acknowledgments

Grateful acknowledgment is made to the editors of the
following journals where some of these poems have appeared:
damn the caesars, Effing, Gam, kadar koli, Mandorla, Skanky Possum,
and *Traverse.*

"The House: A Domestic Novel" first appeared in *Bay Area Poetics,*
edited by Stephanie Young (Faux Press, 2006).

Many thanks to Dale Smith and Hoa Nguyen for publishing
the chapbook *Of Light Reflected* (Skanky Possum, 2001).

The poem "The Morning" was published by John Phillips as
a limited edition chapbook (Given Press, 2002).

"Counterpane" was printed letterpress by the author for the San
Francisco Center for the Book's Poets Pulling Prints Series, 2001.

Special thanks to John Phillips, Hoa Nguyen and Dale Smith,
Richard Owens, Fred Smith and Yasu Esaki, David Hadbawnik,
Elizabeth Robinson, Michael Smoler, Tyler Doherty, Tom Morgan,
and Bootstrap Press.

Poems in *The Morning* are typeset in Californian, originally designed by Frederic Gaudy for a private commission at the University of California, Berkeley in 1939. This digital version was designed by Paul Hunt for the Lanston Type Company. Titles were typeset in Interstate, designed by Tobias Frere-Jones for Font Bureau in 1994.

Book and cover design by Ann Marie Snell. Cover art is *The Day After*, a dry point etching by Yasu Esaki. Digital capture of *The Day After* was provided by Digital Studio, San Francisco.

Printed in an edition of 300 at McNaughton & Gunn, Saline, Michigan.